HONEYBEES

INSECTS

James P. Rowan

The Rourke Corporation, Inc.
Vero Beach, Florida 32964

Edited by Sandra A. Robinson

PHOTO CREDITS
© James P. Rowan: cover, pages 7, 12, 13; © Lynn M. Stone: title
page, pages 18, 21; © Breck Kent: pages 4, 8, 10, 17; © Barry
Mansell: page 15

Library of Congress Cataloging-in-Publication Data

Rowan, James P.
    Honeybees / by James P. Rowan.
        p.   cm. — (The Insect discovery library)
    Includes index.
    Summary: An introduction to the most common species of
honeybee.
    ISBN 0-86593-290-5
    1. Honeybee—Juvenile literature. [1. Honeybee. 2. Bees.]
I. Title. II. Series.
QL568.A6R635   1993
595.79'9—dc20   89-32923
                                                          CIP
                                                          r93

TABLE OF CONTENTS

HONEYBEES

Honeybees are familiar and fascinating insects. They are best-known for producing honey and beeswax.

Honeybees make honey from the sweet liquid, **nectar,** that they collect from flowers. Honeybees gather nectar through their tubelike tongues.

The hind legs of bees have special brushes of stiff, curved hairs. The bee carries tiny grains of flower **pollen** on these hairs.

Female honeybees have a barbed stinger at the far end of their bodies. The stinger is their only weapon for defending themselves and their honey.

A honeybee probes a flower for nectar

KINDS OF BEES

Over 20,000 **species,** or kinds, of bees live over most of the Earth's land surface. Only the honeybee species make enough honey for human use.

The bumblebee is a well-known black and yellow insect. Like honeybees, the big bumblebees are highly **social.** They live together in groups of bees called **colonies,** just as honeybees do.

Leaf-cutting bees are one of many **solitary** bee species. Leaf-cutting bees live alone. They line their nests with pieces of leaves.

A bumblebee visits a blazing-sta for nectar and pollen

HONEYBEE COLONIES

Honeybees live close together and work together. Some colonies of honeybees live in hollow trees. Most colonies live in boxlike shelters built for them by people who raise honeybees. The nesting places are called **hives.**

Honeybees build layers of little wax chambers called honeycomb inside the hive. Each six-sided chamber is called a **cell.** Honeybees store food and raise young bees in the cells.

A beekeeper carefully covers his entire body to avoid stings when he visits a hive

THE QUEEN BEE

Each colony has a queen bee. She is larger and lives longer than the other bees. She may live up to five years. Other bees in the colony, known as workers and **drones,** may live only a few weeks.

The queen's only job is to lay eggs. During her lifetime, she may lay as many as 1 million eggs.

A queen bee (center) has the attention of workers and drones in the hive

Leaf-cutting bees line their nests with leaf pieces

Bald-faced hornets make a ball-shaped paper nest

WORKERS AND DRONES

Most of the 50,000 or more honeybees in a colony are females called workers. They do not produce eggs, but they are truly "busy bees."

At different times, workers clean and guard the hive, produce beeswax, care for young bees and gather nectar. Workers also feed the male bees, or drones.

The drones' only job is to fly to another hive and mate with the queen there. The drones die each fall when the workers force them from the hive.

One of the worker bee's many jobs is to guard the nest against honey-hungry black bears

FROM EGG TO ADULT

The queen bee lays eggs in the cells of the hive. The wormlike young that hatch are called larvas. Within five days, the squiggly larvas enter the **pupa,** or resting, stage of their lives. Workers close their cells with wax. In less than two weeks, the pupas become adults.

A few larvas are fed a special, steady diet of "royal jelly" by worker bees. These larvas become queens.

Queen (center left) lays all of the colony's eggs

HONEYBEE TALK

Honeybees don't really talk, but they do tell each other things. A worker bee can tell other bees in the hive about its discovery of flowers rich in nectar. The messenger bee does a special dance in the hive. The type of dance tells the other workers where the flowers are. Flower odors on the bee tell the others the kind of flower the worker has found.

When she returns to the hive, the worker can let the whole colony know where this purple milkweed is

"KILLER" BEES AND WASPS

"Killer" bees are closely related to common honeybees. However, killer bees are much more likely to attack and sting. **Swarms** of angry killer bees have stung large animals to death—and even have killed people in Central and South America. Moving northward, killer bees have just begun to reach Texas.

Wasps and hornets are cousins of bees. They share many of the same habits and body parts.

Certain wasps and hornets build paper nests by chewing up wood and mixing it with water and saliva.

Paper wasps produce their own brand of paper for nest-building

HONEYBEES AND PEOPLE

Some people fear all bees because of their stingers. Only people who are allergic to bee stings, however, have much to fear. They should always carry medicine in case they are stung.

Honeybees are useful because they produce honey and beeswax. It's even more important that they carry pollen on their bodies from one plant to another. The exchange of pollen helps plants reproduce.

Many of the plants that bees **pollinate** are important for human food.

Glossary

cell (SELL) — any of the small, six-sided chambers in which bees store food and raise young

colony (KAHL uh nee) — a group of nesting animals of the same kind

drone (DRONE) — male honeybees

hive (HIVE) — the place in which bees nest, produce honey and raise young

nectar (NEK ter) — a sweet liquid made by flowers

pollen (PAHL in) — dustlike grains produced by flowers; pollen is needed for flower reproduction

pollinate (PAHL uh nate) — to move pollen from one plant to another

pupa (PYU puh) — the stage of development between larva and adult when the insect is inactive

social (SO shul) — spending considerable time in the company of others of the same kind

solitary (SAHL uh tar ee) — alone

species (SPEE sheez) — within a group of closely-related living things, such as bees, one certain kind or type (*bumble*bee)

swarm (SWORM) — a great, buzzing mass of bees

INDEX